I0815327

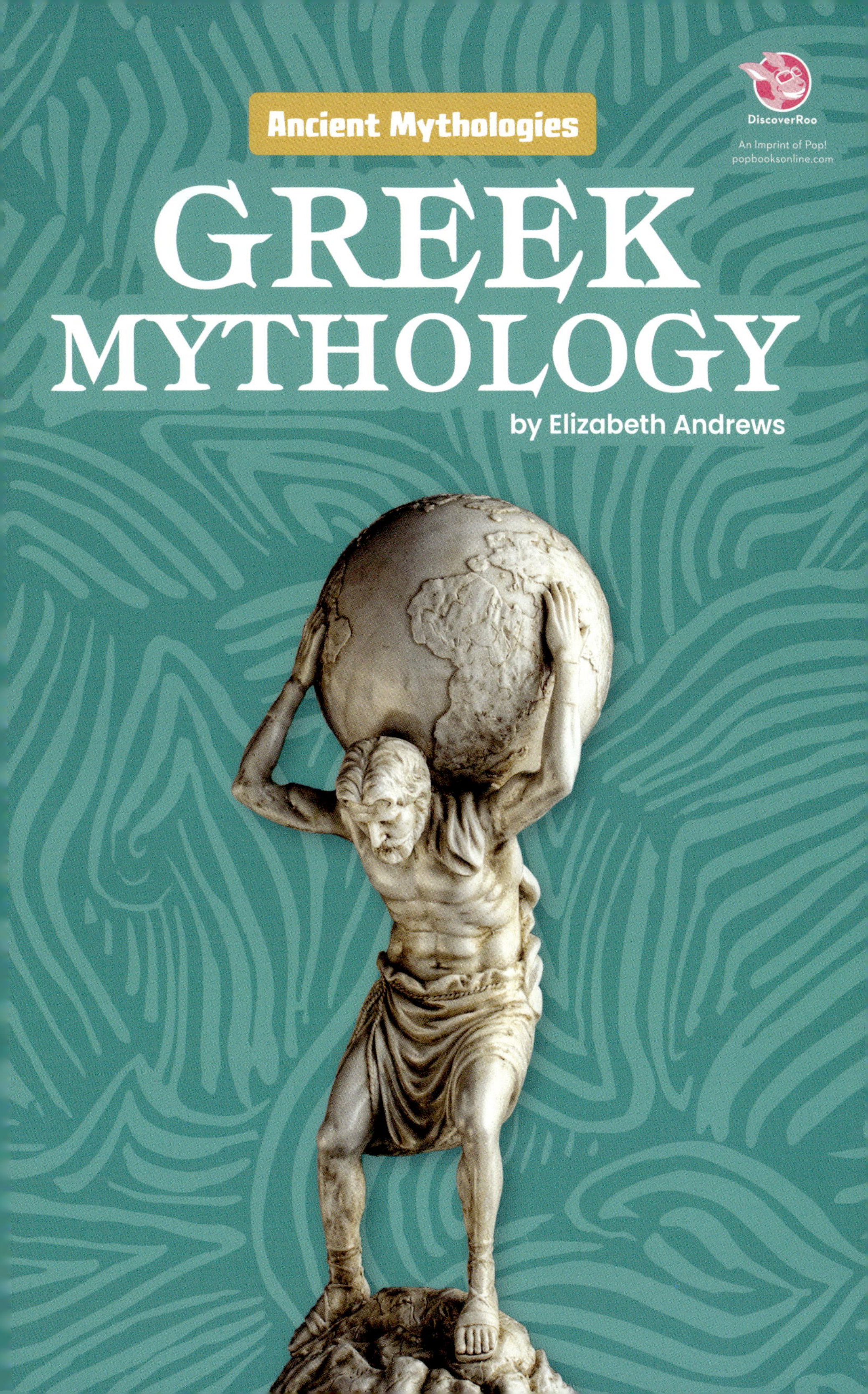
Ancient Mythologies
GREEK MYTHOLOGY
by Elizabeth Andrews
DiscoverRoo
An Imprint of Pop!
popbooksonline.com

This book is filled with videos, puzzles, games, and more! Scan the QR codes* while you read, or visit the website below to make this book pop.

popbooksonline.com/greek-myth

abdobooks.com
Published by Pop!, a division of ABDO, PO Box 398166, Minneapolis, Minnesota 55439.

Printed in the United States of America, North Mankato, Minnesota.

102024
012025

Cover Photo: Shutterstock Images
Interior Photos: Getty Images, Shutterstock Images, Wikimedia Commons
Editor: Krissy Sterling
Series Designer: Colleen McLaren

Library of Congress Control Number: 2024938636

Publisher's Cataloging-in-Publication Data
Names: Andrews, Elizabeth, author.
Title: Greek mythology / by Elizabeth Andrews
Description: Minneapolis, Minnesota : Pop!, 2025 | Series: Ancient mythologies | Includes online resources and index
Identifiers: ISBN 9781098247034 (lib. bdg.) | ISBN 9781098247591 (ebook)
Subjects: LCSH: Mythology--Juvenile literature. | Mythology, Greek--Juvenile literature. | Gods, Greek--Juvenile literature. | Deities--Juvenile literature. | Mythology, European--Juvenile literature.
Classification: DDC 292.1--dc23

*Scanning QR codes requires a web-enabled smart device with a QR code reader app and a camera.

TABLE OF CONTENTS

CHAPTER 1

FIRST THERE WAS CHAOS

Before there was anything, there was Chaos. Gaia, or Mother Earth, was born from the dark nothingness of Chaos. Gaia created Uranus, the father of the sky. Together they had 12 children. They were called the Titans. Titans were giant and powerful.

WATCH A VIDEO HERE!

The Titans overthrew their parents. A Titan named Cronus became the world's first king. Cronus and his wife Rhea had six children who were gods. Cronus worried his children would **betray** him like he betrayed his own father. To prevent this, he swallowed each child after it was born.

Cronus was the youngest of the twelve Titans.

Zeus grew up on the island of Crete.

When Rhea had her last child, Zeus, she tricked Cronus into swallowing a rock wrapped in a blanket instead of the baby. Zeus grew up. He found a way to make Cronus throw up all his siblings. Then he challenged the Titans to war and won. The Titans were trapped in the underworld. Zeus and the gods and goddesses who fought with him became the Olympians.

One Titan was saved from the underworld. His name was Prometheus. Zeus asked him to create humans. Prometheus shaped people out of mud and the goddess Athena breathed life into them. However, Prometheus disobeyed Zeus and gave humans fire. Fire was only meant for the gods.

Zeus had Prometheus chained to a rock. An eagle eats his liver every day.

Zeus punished Prometheus and the humans by sending a beautiful woman named Pandora to them. Zeus gave Pandora a box and told her not to open it. But she did open it. Evils, such as disease, hunger, pain, and death were released

Pandora had a jar instead of a box in some versions of this myth.

into the world. In the end, only hope remained in the box. Now, hope is the most important thing humans have to survive the evils.

Nearly every society has a myth about human creation. Myths are stories that often involve gods and **supernatural** events. They are not always based on facts. Myths helped people make sense of the world around them.

ATHENA

Zeus was first married to a nymph named Metis. She helped Zeus save his siblings. Metis predicted that one of Zeus's children would overthrow him. Zeus worried this was true, so when Metis became pregnant, he swallowed her. The child Metis was carrying kept growing. Eventually, the goddess Athena was born from Zeus's head. Athena became his favorite child.

CHAPTER 2

GODS AND GODDESSES

Zeus is the god of the sky and King of the Olympians. He has five siblings. They are Hades, Hera, Hestia, Demeter, and Poseidon.

Hades rules the underworld. Hera is the goddess of women and marriage. Demeter is the goddess of the harvest.

LEARN MORE HERE!

She is very important to ancient Greeks. Poseidon rules the sea. Hestia is the goddess of the **hearth** fire and home.

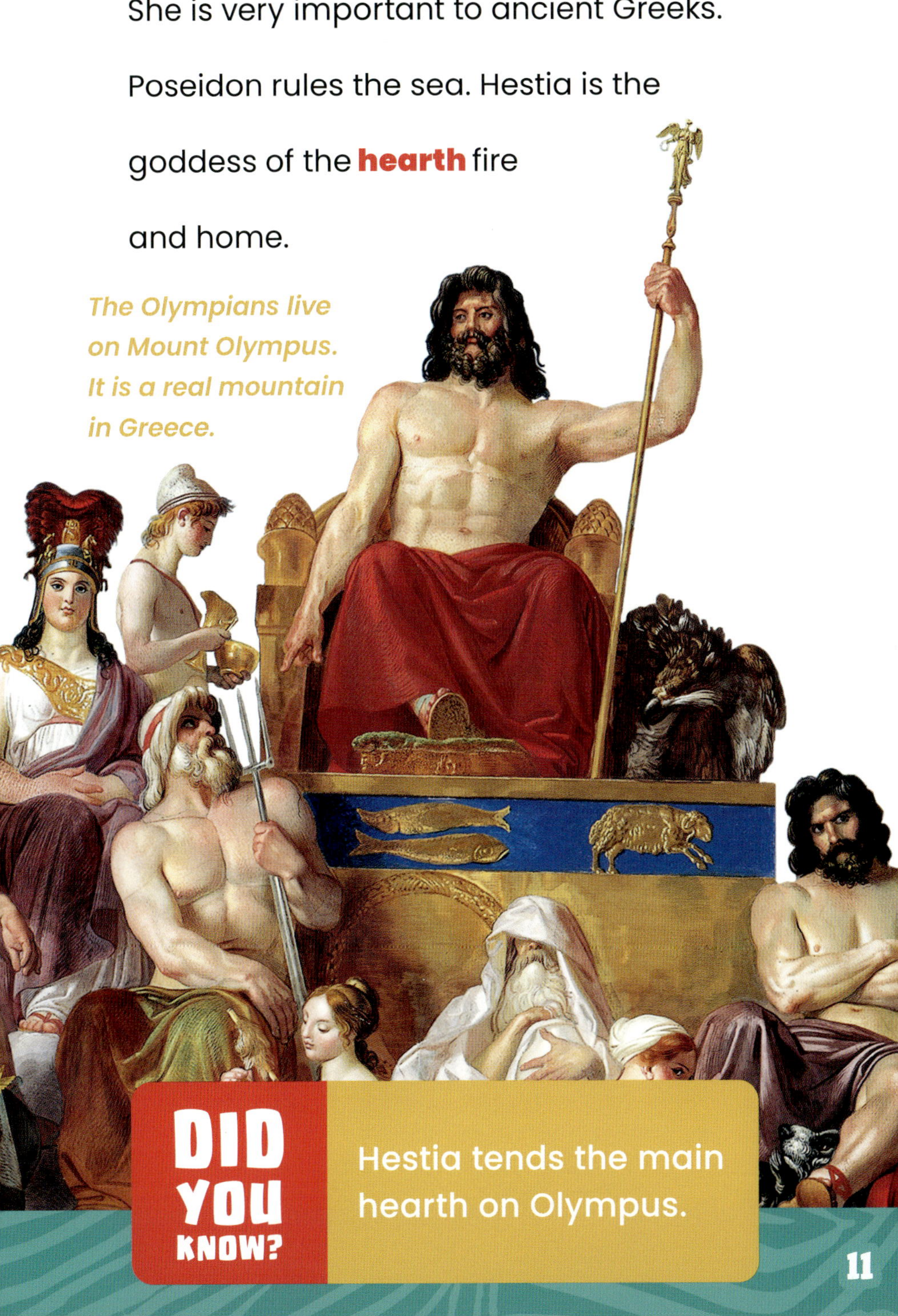

The Olympians live on Mount Olympus. It is a real mountain in Greece.

DID YOU KNOW?

Hestia tends the main hearth on Olympus.

Along with Zeus and his siblings, six other gods and goddesses are considered Olympians. They are the children of Zeus. Zeus married Hera. But he is known to have relationships and children with others. Hera often feels **jealous** and angry.

Some of Ares's symbols are a helmet, armor, and dog.

Zeus and Hera had Ares, the god of war, and Hephaestus, the god of the forge. The other Olympians are Aphrodite, the goddess of love and beauty and Athena, the goddess of wisdom and war. Hermes is messenger to the gods. Apollo is the god of music, archery, and **oracles**. His twin sister Artemis is the goddess of the hunt and wild things.

Hephaestus makes all the weapons for the Olympians.

PANTHEON

All Greek gods and goddesses are a part of the Greek Pantheon. The Pantheon is ruled by the Olympians.

There are many other gods and goddesses in Greek mythology. Some married the children of other Olympians. Each one has their own story and purpose.

Persephone is Demeter's daughter and Hades's wife. Hades stole her from her mother. Demeter was so sad she let all the plants die. Hades agreed to return Persephone for six months each year. When Persephone spends spring and summer on earth, nature thrives. During fall and winter, she lives in the underworld. This story explained why things die in the fall and winter.

CHAPTER 3

MYTHICAL BEINGS

The gods often have relationships and children with humans. These children are known as demigods. Some **inherit** the powers of their godly parents. They go on incredible adventures. Hercules is a demigod. He is famous for his strength and ability to do hard things.

EXPLORE LINKS HERE!

Hercules defeated the centaur who stole his wife.

Nymphs kidnapped Hercules's servant Hylas because he was so handsome.

The Greeks believed all things in nature contain and are protected by a female spirit called a nymph. Nereids are nymphs who live in seas. Naiads

DID YOU KNOW?

The war hero Achilles's mother was a nereid.

live in fresh water. Dryads live in forests and trees. Nymphs also fall in love with humans. Their children often grow up to be important kings and heroes.

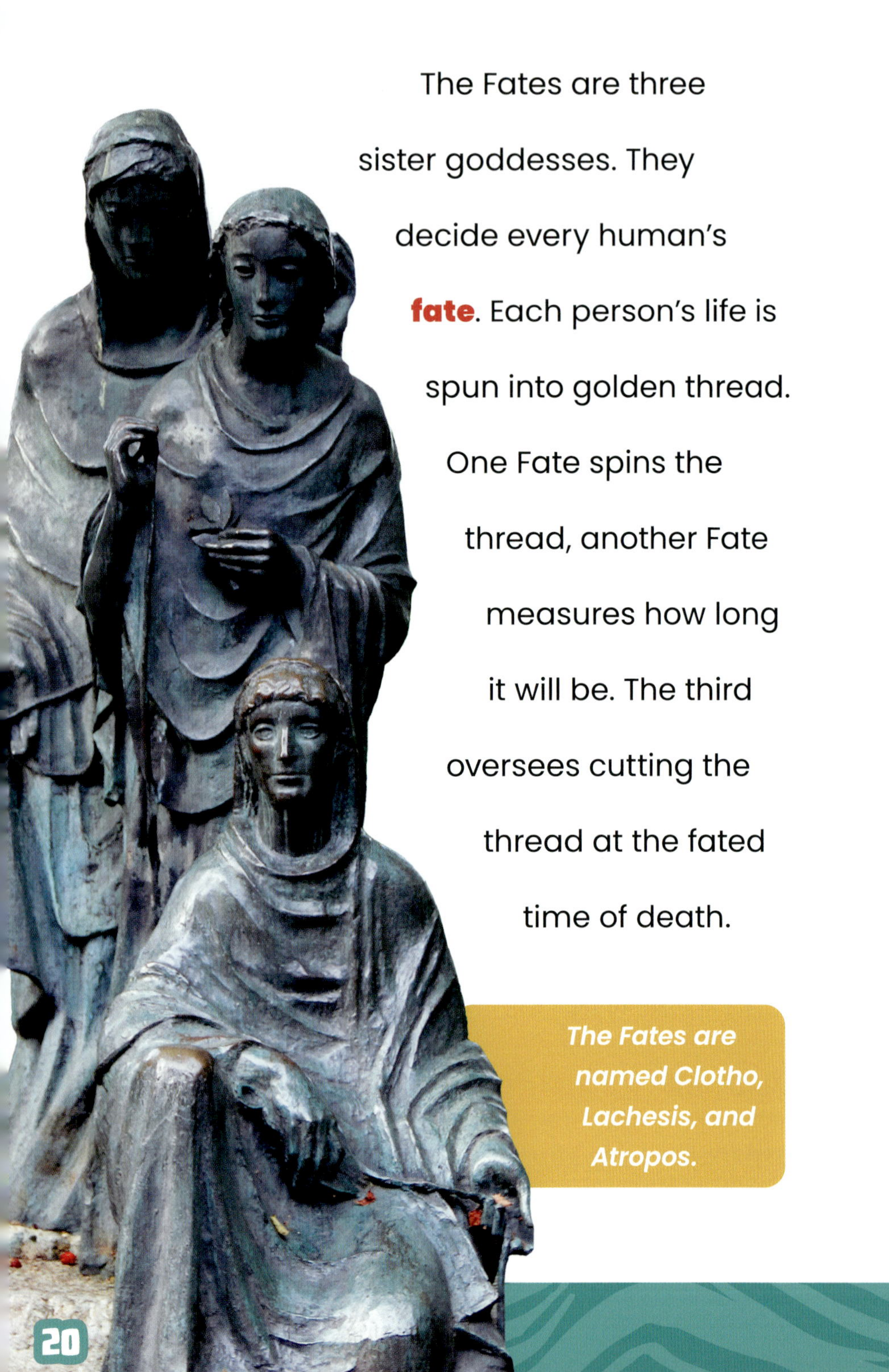

The Fates are three sister goddesses. They decide every human's **fate**. Each person's life is spun into golden thread. One Fate spins the thread, another Fate measures how long it will be. The third oversees cutting the thread at the fated time of death.

The Fates are named Clotho, Lachesis, and Atropos.

The Minotaur was slayed by the demigod Theseus. He was a hero.

There are also monsters and beasts in Greek mythology. The Minotaur lives in a **labyrinth**. He has the body of a man and the head of a bull. The Chimera is a combination of a lion, goat, and giant snake. Pegasus is a beautiful horse with wings and magical powers.

CHAPTER 4

HEROES AND MONSTERS

Greek mythology is full of stories about heroes overcoming the odds. Many problems they face are created by the gods. Greek gods and goddesses often play with humans as though they are toys. One of the most famous stories of this occurs during the Trojan War.

COMPLETE AN ACTIVITY HERE!

Phaethon was a demigod who tried to drive the chariot that pulls the sun across the sky. He brought the sun too close to the earth and Zeus had to shoot him down.

Paris stole Helen from Menelaus, the King of Sparta.

Hera, Aphrodite, and Athena were fighting about which of them was most beautiful. They made the human prince of Troy, Paris, choose. He chose Aphrodite. To thank him, Aphrodite promised him Helen.

Helen was the most beautiful woman in the world. However, she was already married to a Greek king. Paris stole her away. This started a war between the Trojans and the Greeks.

Aphrodite was born from the foam in the sea.

Heroes of the Trojan War were Menelaus, Paris, Diomedes, Odysseus, Nestor, Achilles, and Agamemnon.

Many gods and goddesses chose sides in this war. Hera and Athena were upset Aphrodite was named the most beautiful. They supported the Greeks. Aphrodite and Ares sided with the Trojans. The gods offered some soldiers divine favors. For a while, the Trojans were winning.

Odysseus, a Greek soldier, came up with a plan to sneak into the city of Troy. The Greeks built a large wooden horse with the help of Athena. It was offered as a gift of surrender to the Trojans. They brought it into the city. Little did they know, Greek soldiers hid inside. When the Greeks escaped, they took over the city and won the war.

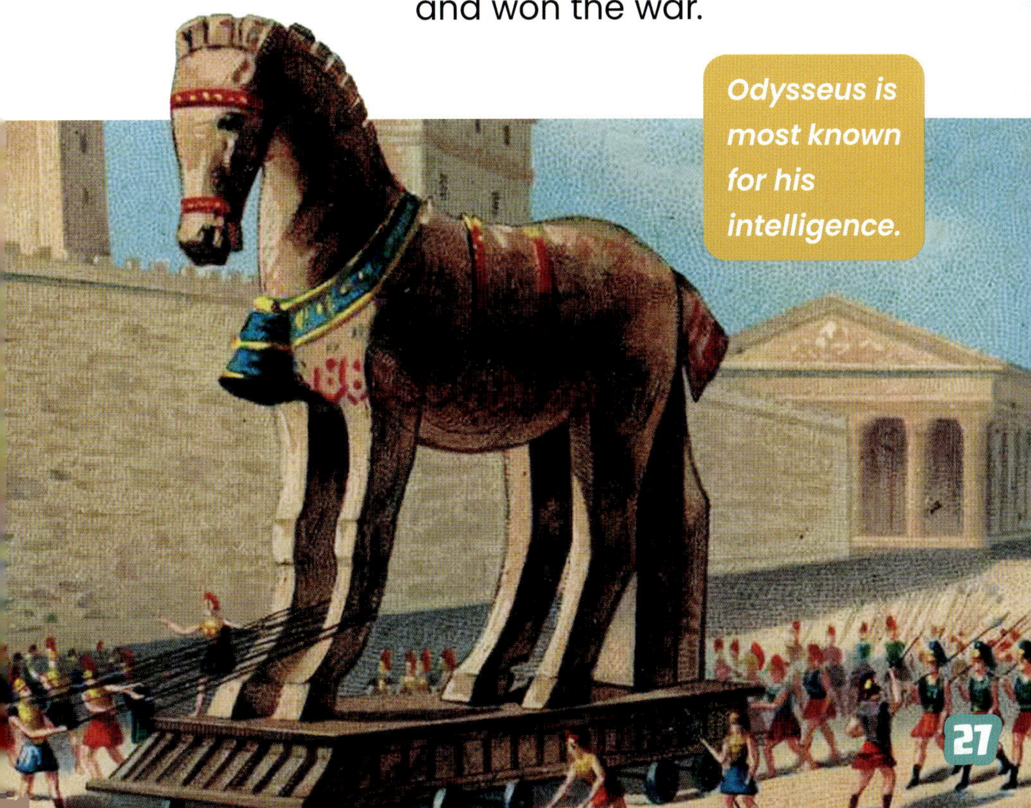

Odysseus is most known for his intelligence.

When Odysseus sailed home after the war, he encountered all kinds of mythical beings. He met the witch Circe, escaped an island of **cyclopes**, sailed through dangerous **whirlpools**, and escaped a six-headed female snake monster. Athena helped Odysseus on his journey home.

Odysseus and his men sailed past an island of sirens. Their beautiful songs often lead sailors to crash their ships.

Athena fought alongside Achilles during the Trojan War.

Today, stories from Greek mythology inspire shows, books, art, and more. The Percy Jackson series is loved by young readers around the world. Disney released a movie following part of the story of Hercules.

The story of the Trojan War and Odysseus's journey home are written as epic poems called the *Iliad* and the *Odyssey*.

MAKING CONNECTIONS

TEXT-TO-SELF

If you lived at the time of ancient Greeks, which god or goddess do you think you would have worshipped? Please explain why.

TEXT-TO-TEXT

Have you read any other books about ancient mythologies? If so, what did those mythologies have in common with Greek myths?

TEXT-TO-WORLD

Greek mythology is still mentioned in books, TV shows, movies, and music. With the help of an adult, look up pieces of entertainment inspired by Greek mythology. Write a short paragraph about what you found and which myths are referenced.

GLOSSARY

betray — to not remain loyal or faithful to.

cyclopes — giants in Greek mythology who have only one eye in the middle of their foreheads.

fate — the power that is often believed to decide what will happen in human life.

hearth — the floor of a fireplace.

inherit — to receive through a parent's genes.

jealous — feeling envy over what another person has or can do.

labyrinth — a complicated maze.

oracle — a person dedicated to serving a god or goddess. They often give predictions and warnings for the future.

supernatural — having to do with forces beyond what is natural.

whirlpool — water turning rapidly about a center and pulling downward.

INDEX

DiscoverRoo!
ONLINE RESOURCES

This book is filled with videos, puzzles, games, and more! Scan the QR codes* while you read, or visit the website below to make this book pop.

popbooksonline.com/greek-myth

*Scanning QR codes requires a web-enabled smart device with a QR code reader app and a camera.